A DAY THAT MADE HISTORY

PEARL HARBOR

Nathaniel Harris

Dryad Press Limited   London

F

Contents

Acknowledgments

The author and publishers thank the following for their kind permission to reproduce copyright illustrations: Bettmann Archive, pages 24, 44, 46, 62; Blandford Press, pages 7, 8; BBC Hulton Picture Library, pages 41, 56; Robert Hunt Library, pages 14 (bottom), 39, 42, 58; Imperial War Museum, pages 25, 30, 34, 57; The Mansell Collection, page 38; The Photo Source, page 61; Popperfoto, page 36; The Research House/US Navy, cover; Franklin D. Roosevelt Library, page 16 (top); US National Archives, pages 14 (top), 16 (bottom), 22, 48, 52, 55, 59; US Naval Institute, page 6; US Navy, pages 4, 60. The maps on pages 10-11 and 21 are by R.F. Brien. The pictures were researched by David Pratt.

The "Day that Made History" series was devised by Nathaniel Harris.

To Ruth Taylor, who prompted

Typeset by Tek-Art Ltd, Kent, and printed in Great Britain by R.J. Acford, Chichester for the publishers, Dryad Press Limited, 4 Fitzhardinge Street, London W1H 0AH

ISBN 0 8521 9669 5

21123714L

TJ

THE
EVENTS

"This can't be true!"

In Washington, D.C., it was just after half-past one in the afternoon of Sunday, 7th December, 1941. In the Navy Building on Constitution Avenue, the United States Secretary of the Navy, Frank Knox, stood talking to the Chief of Naval Operations and two of their assistants. Then a naval commander appeared and handed Knox a radio message. It read: AIR RAID PEARL HARBOR. THIS IS NOT A DRILL.

"My God," cried Knox in astonishment, "this can't be true – this must mean the Philippines." He had no doubt that the attackers were Japanese, but for a moment he refused to believe that they could have struck halfway across the Pacific Ocean at the great American base on Oahu, one of the Hawaiian Islands. Nevertheless the message was clearly marked: it came direct from the commander of the Pacific Fleet stationed at Pearl Harbor.

Knox immediately telephoned the news to the White House. It reached President Roosevelt at 1:40 in the Oval Office, where he was talking to his adviser, Harry Hopkins. The President also questioned the accuracy of the signal at first; earlier in the day he had assured his physician – a navy man – that "Japan's military masters would not risk a war with the United States." But now, when Hopkins was told, and insisted that "there must be some mistake", Roosevelt disagreed. He had already realized that it was "just the kind of unexpected thing the Japanese would do". Conscious that Japanese-American talks were still going on, he added bitterly that "At the very time they were discussing peace in the Pacific they were plotting to overthrow it."

Meanwhile, at Pearl Harbor in the Central Pacific it was not yet 8:30 in the morning, and the second wave of Japanese planes was about to arrive, intent on finishing off the American fleet. Despite their use of air patrols and radar, the Americans had failed to identify the enemy before he fell on them, destroying most of their planes on the ground and bombing the fleet almost at will. Thanks to a combination of audacity, meticulous planning and sheer good luck – helped by American shortcomings – the Japanese had achieved one of the most devastating military surprises in history.

Yamamoto's plan

A plan takes shape

The basic reason for the attack on Pearl Harbor was simple: Japan wanted to conquer large areas of Asia, and the United States stood in her way. Britain, France and Holland possessed substantial colonies in Asia and would also normally have opposed the Japanese; but by 1940 they were preoccupied with the war in Europe launched by Hitler's Germany. By contrast, the United States was still at peace, had army and airforce bases in the Philippines – and had stationed her mighty Pacific Fleet at Pearl Harbor, on Oahu in the Hawaiian Islands, where it was in a position to intervene against any move made by the Japanese. Talks between Japan and the United States continued, but many people in both countries believed that war was inevitable.

Among them was Admiral Isoroku Yamamoto, Commander-in-Chief of the Imperial Japanese Combined Fleet. Yamamoto was a thickset bulldog of a man in his late fifties, tough, outspoken, domineering – and a compulsive gambler with a passion for poker and bridge.

It was Yamamoto who conceived the daring scheme to cross the Pacific and destroy the US Pacific Fleet in a surprise attack on the mighty island fortress of Oahu. Yamamoto realized that this would not defeat the Americans; in fact, having worked in the United States, he knew that Japan could never match American military and industrial power, and he thought that it would be folly to plunge into a war. But if Japan's leaders *did* decide to fight, an attack on Pearl Harbor was the best chance. The destruction of the US Pacific Fleet would give the Japanese a breathing-space in which to bring off their long-planned "Southern Operation" – the conquest of South-East Asia – and to build up their empire against an eventual American counter-attack. Towards the end of 1940, when the Japanese prime minister asked him about the chances of success if a war should break out, Yamamoto answered candidly, "If I am told to fight regardless of the consequences, I shall run wild for the first six months or a year, but I have absolutely no confidence about the second and third year."

Most Navy chiefs were against Yamamoto's proposed

◁ *The attack on Pearl Harbor was conceived and ordered by Admiral Isoroku Yamamoto, Commander-in-Chief of the Imperial Japanese Combined Fleet. Off duty, Yamamoto was a notorious gambler: the attack was his greatest gamble – and one that came off.*

attack, arguing that it involved terrible risks to ships, planes and men that Japan could not afford to lose. Yamamoto understood the dangers ("We must be prepared to risk complete annihilation"), but insisted that his was the only way. The plan could only be carried out if his superiors authorized it, but there was nothing to stop Yamamoto making all the preparations; and that is exactly what he did during the spring and summer of 1941, while Japan and the United States negotiated with increasingly remote prospects of reaching agreement.

Solving the problems

The main offensive weapon to be used against Pearl Harbor was a relatively new one: warplanes transported to within range of the target by aircraft carriers and then launched from their decks. These, Yamamoto believed, could destroy not only the enemy's carriers, but also his battleships – the mighty-gunned, armour-plated "battlewaggons" that were still regarded by most sailors as the pride of every navy. Foreseeing that mastery of the air would be decisive in future wars, Yamamoto realized that carriers had become as important as battleships to the survival of a fleet – and especially a fleet operating in the vastness of the Pacific, far beyond the range of land-based aircraft. The largest possible number of carriers, holding the largest possible number of planes and escorted by a powerful group of warships, might cross the Pacific until they were close enough for the Japanese planes to attack the US Pacific Fleet.

This apparently simple scheme entailed all sorts of difficulties. By February 1941 many of these had been ironed out by the Navy's greatest expert on air power, Commander Minoru Genda, whom Yamamoto had ordered to produce a detailed, workable plan. Luckily for Genda, he had plenty of information about Pearl Harbor and Oahu, thanks to Japanese spies posing as employees of the Japanese consulate on the island. He knew the layout of the harbour, with its mile-wide southern entrance opening into an irregularly-shaped stretch of shallow water with an island – Ford Island – in the middle. He had much useful information about the carriers, cruisers, destroyers and other vessels that thronged the harbour. He knew that the Americans habitually double-berthed their battleships on the eastern side of Ford Island. He knew where the airfields were. And above all he knew that

Commander Minoru Genda, who was responsible for the detailed planning of the attack on Pearl Harbor.

the Americans were careless enough to follow a regular routine: the Fleet returned to port for the weekend, and after a heavy Saturday night there was little activity in Pearl Harbor on a Sunday morning – which made that the ideal time for the Japanese to strike. Annoyingly, the least predictable ship movements were those of the "flattops" – the carriers, which Genda, like Yamamoto, regarded as of vital importance in the approaching war.

By the early summer of 1941, flyers of the Japanese First Air Fleet had begun an intensive training. By September this had become highly specialized, as the crews of high-level bombers, dive-bombers, torpedo-bombers and fighters were prepared for their different roles in the operation – without their suspecting that they were all part of a single plan, let alone an intended attack on Pearl Harbor.

As Yamamoto and Genda meant them to be, the Japanese flyers became a crack force, with the kind of accuracy and instant reflexes required by their mission. The fighter-pilots achieved this fairly easily: their machines were the new and advanced Zeros, which had already proved their worth in combat over China. But the Japanese bombers did not produce the kind of results necessary to make Yamamoto's plan a success until nerve-wrackingly late in the day. The emphasis throughout was on improved performance even where this involved serious risks. The dive-bombers improved their accuracy by learning to swoop down to 450

The Mitsubishi Zero-sen, the famous Japanese fighter which dominated the skies over Pearl Harbor. It was in effect a Japanese secret weapon, tested in combat over China but virtually unknown to the Americans and British. Its speed (up to about 560 kph) and manoeuvrability ensured its supremacy throughout 1941-2.

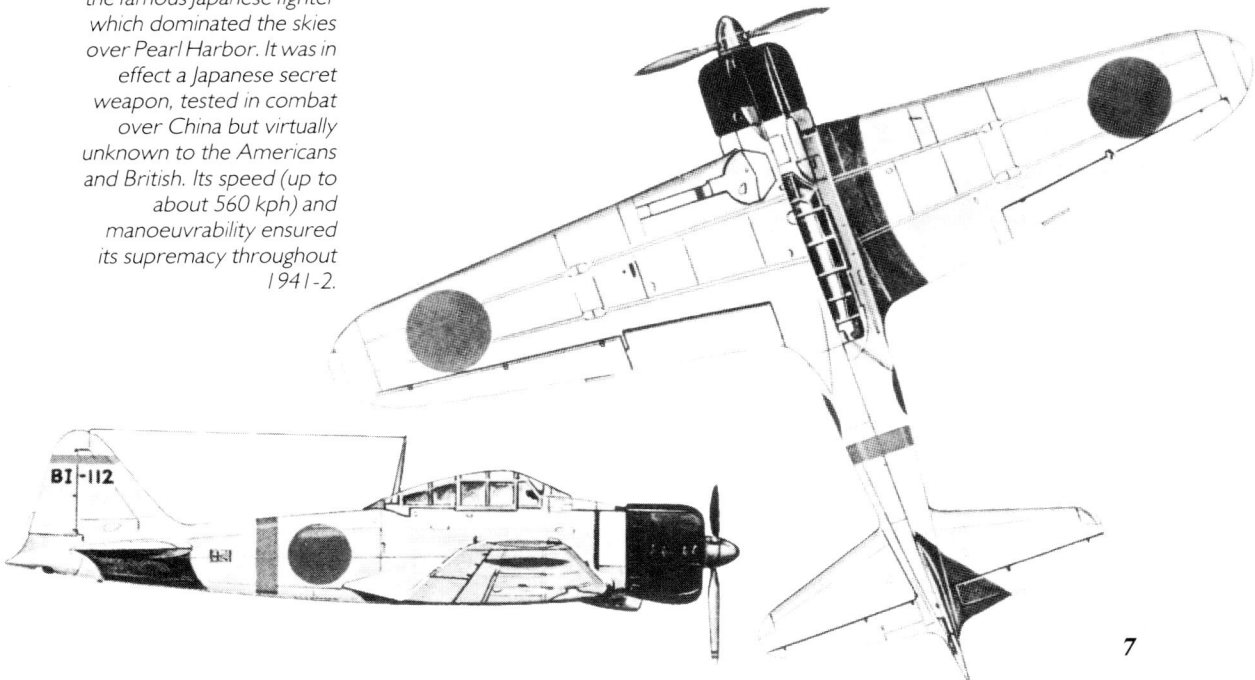

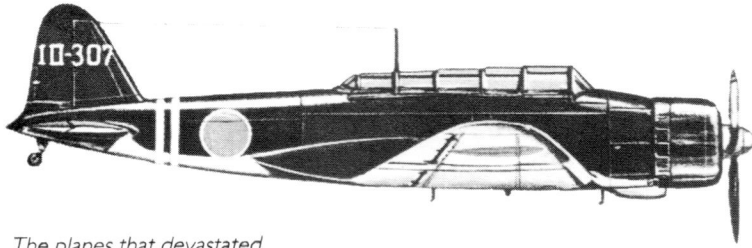

The planes that devastated the American Pacific Fleet. Above: The Nakajima B5N2, nicknamed "Kate", carried torpedoes specially adapted to run through the shallow waters of Pearl Harbor. It was also used for the high-level bombing during the operation. Right: The Aichi D3A1, or "Val", dive-bomber also played a vital role in the attack.

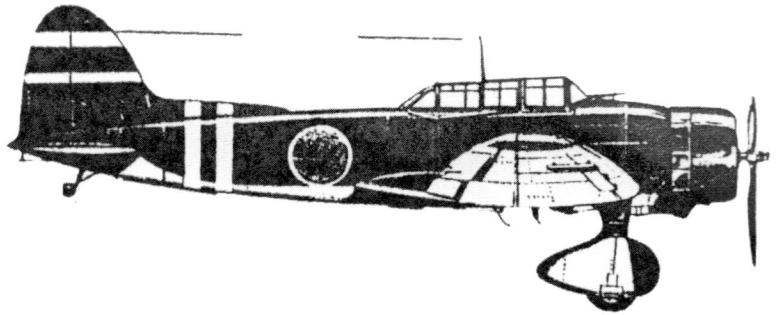

metres (instead of 600) before releasing their missiles; at that height, it was discovered, they could still just manage to pull out of their dive without crashing. The high-level bombers improved their accuracy by dropping their loads from a lower altitude – 3,000 metres instead of 4,000 or even 5,000 – although this made them far more vulnerable to anti-aircraft fire. Such a change was only possible because the Japanese had developed a more powerful bomb; the previous model had needed the momentum acquired during a 4,000-metre drop if it was to pierce the armoured decks of a battleship.

The most serious of all Genda's problems was solved by a similar technical breakthrough. The problem was created by the shallowness of the water in Pearl Harbor, which was, on average, a mere 12 metres deep. With so little margin for error, no torpedo fired from a plane would keep on a sufficiently level course to avoid sticking in the mud before it reached its target. Yet the torpedo-bombers were the key factor in the Japanese plan: they were earmarked to blast holes in the relatively vulnerable sides of the US battleships. The dive-bombers would not be able to penetrate the thick deck armour of the battlewaggons (their missiles were too light), and so if the torpedo programme turned out to be impractical the task of destroying the battleships would be borne entirely by the high-level bombers, which could hardly score as many hits at 3,000 metres as the torpedo planes could at close range.

Luckily for the Japanese, frantic experimental work produced a new model of torpedo with a stabilizing fin that worked in less than 12 metres of water. At once the manufacturing firm of Mitsubishi began to make equally frantic efforts to produce enough of the new torpedoes in time.

Yamamoto's ultimatum

By mid-October 1941 Japanese war planning was far advanced. Essentially, the preparations were for the "Southern Operation", involving a multi-pronged invasion of South-East Asia. Yamamoto's plan, though discussed and debated at length, failed to convince the makers of policy on the Naval General Staff. Then, on 18th October, the Admiral sent the General Staff a message: if his plan was not adopted, he could no longer be responsible for the security of the Japanese Empire – and he and his entire staff would feel compelled to resign. Was Yamamoto, the poker-player, bluffing? We shall never know, since – if it was a bluff – no one dared to call it. Alarmed by the prospect of losing their most famous commander just when war was about to break out, the General Staff referred the matter to the Minister for the Navy, and he authorized Yamamoto to go ahead. The Southern Operation and the Pearl Harbor plan would be carried out – and, for maximum impact, at the same time. Japan would attack to the south and the east simultaneously, synchronizing her operations over 6,000 miles of ocean.

None of this was known to the Japanese flyers, training hard on Kyushu, the southernmost of Japan's four main islands. Yet the operation was timed to begin only a month later. By 17th November, a task force of Japanese ships had assembled at Saeki Bay, on the west coast of Kyushu, and had taken the selected flyers and planes on board. Security remained tight, and even now, most of the sailors and flyers had no idea where they were going. To the last, the Japanese were racing against the clock; the final consignment of the new torpedoes was only just delivered in time, and one of the carriers stayed on after the rest had left, to take them on board. Late in the afternoon, after a last briefing from Yamamoto, the ships slipped away one by one, each making her way separately and unobtrusively to the chosen rendezvous.

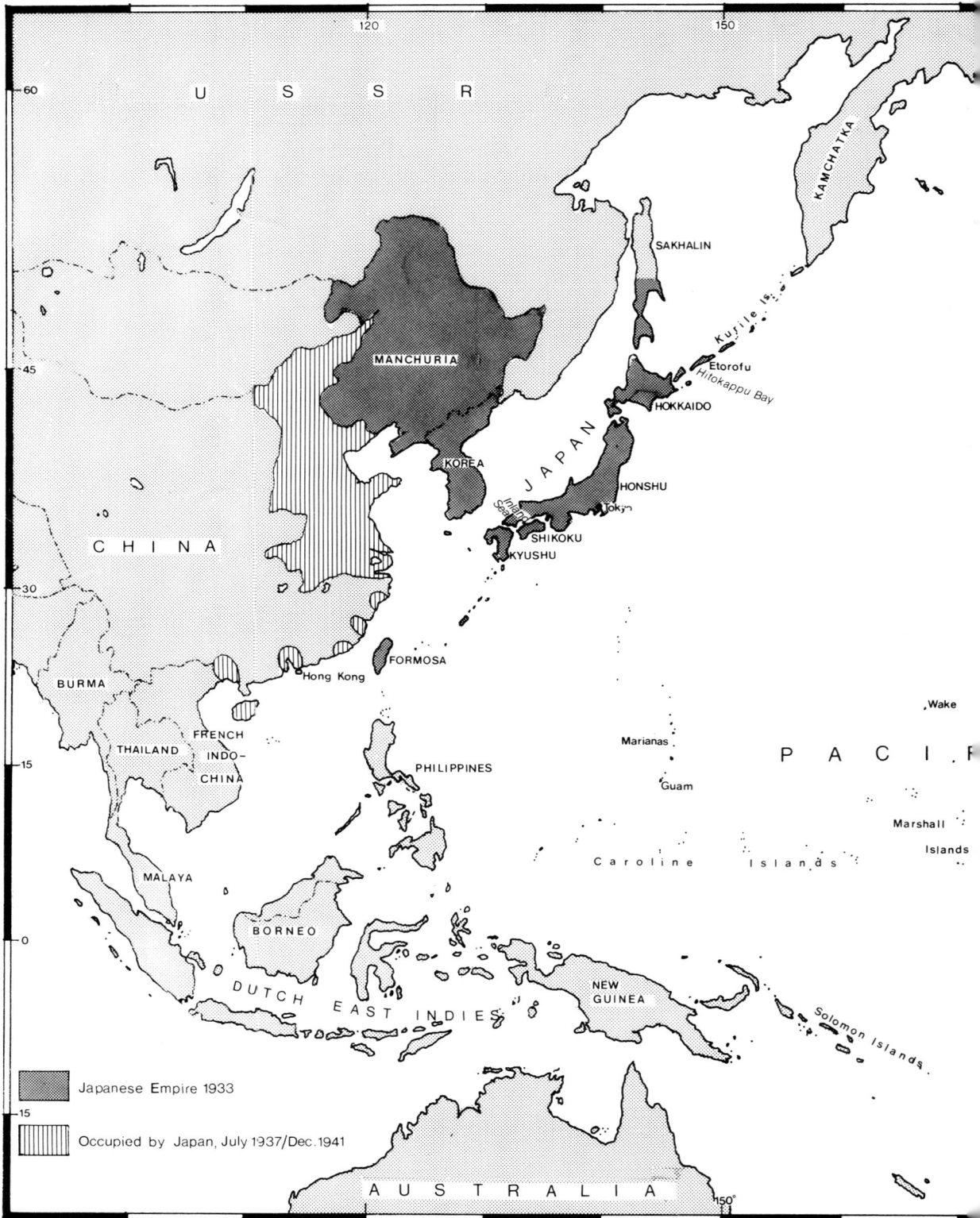

USSR

KAMCHATKA

SAKHALIN

MANCHURIA

Kurile Is.
Etorofu
Hitokappu Bay

HOKKAIDO

KOREA

JAPAN

HONSHU

Tokyo

Inland Sea
SHIKOKU
KYUSHU

CHINA

BURMA

Hong Kong

FORMOSA

THAILAND
FRENCH INDO-CHINA

PHILIPPINES

Marianas

Guam

Wake

P A C I F

Marshall

Islands

C a r o l i n e   I s l a n d s

MALAYA

BORNEO

D U T C H   E A S T   I N D I E S

NEW GUINEA

Solomon Islands

A U S T R A L I A

Japanese Empire 1933

Occupied by Japan, July 1937/Dec.1941

Mercator's projection

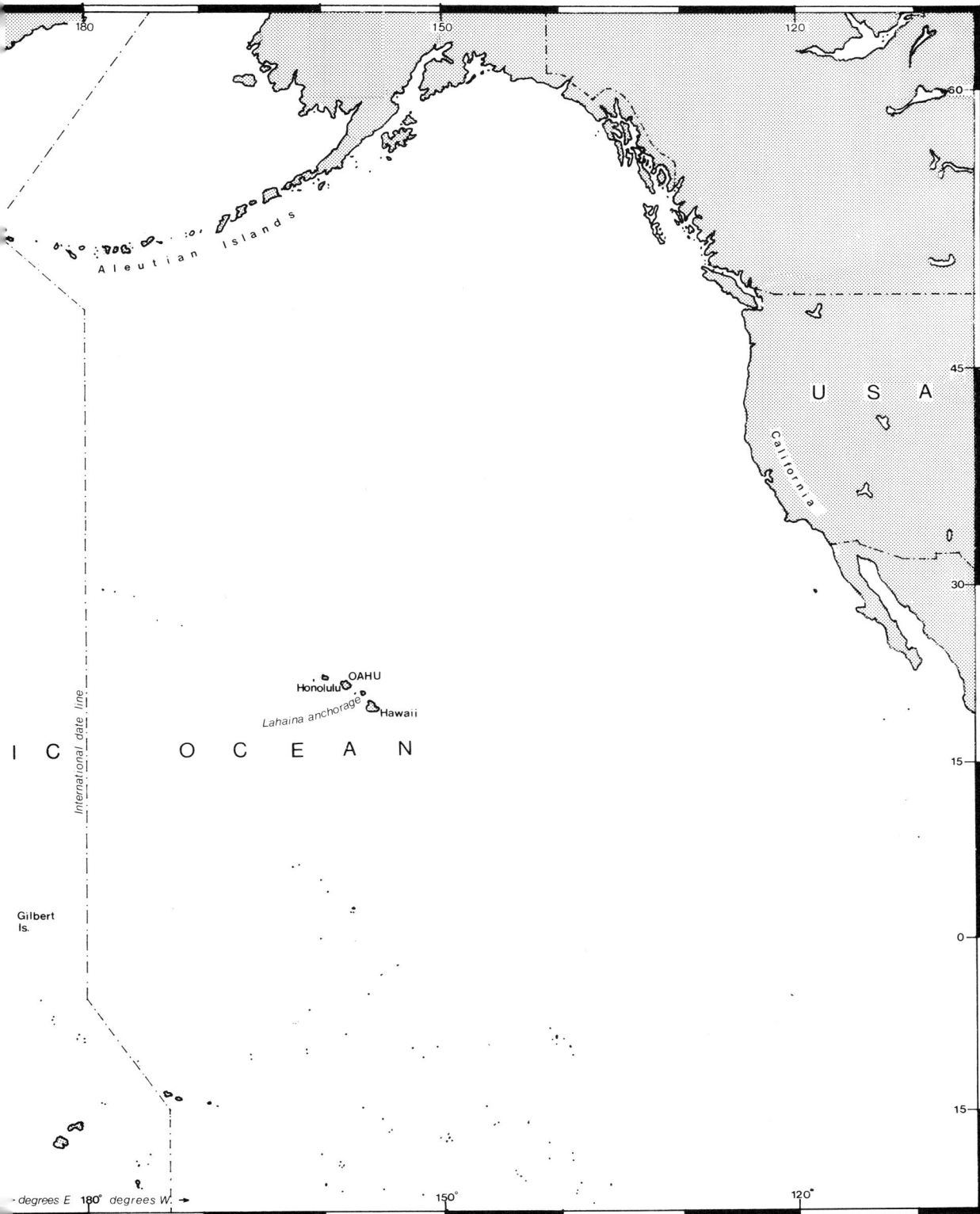

180
150
120
60
45
USA
California
30
A l e u t i a n   I s l a n d s
International date line
OAHU
Honolulu
Lahaina anchorage
Hawaii
I C
O C E A N
15
Gilbert
Is.
0
15
degrees E 180° degrees W. →
150°
120°

Under way

The task force

By 22nd November all the Japanese ships had reached the rendezvous. This was Hitokappu Bay, on Etorofu, one of the Kurile Islands. The Kuriles consisted of 32 little islands, strung out like a necklace chain between Japan and Soviet Kamchatka and inhabited mainly by a small population of hunters and fishermen. This mistily remote location virtually guaranteed that the task force would not be spotted while it assembled in readiness for its voyage across the Pacific.

As commander of the Combined Fleet, responsible for the Southern Operation as well as Pearl Harbor, Yamamoto could not take personal charge of the task force. The job was given to Vice-Admiral Chuichi Nagumo, an officer who was prepared to do his duty but who took a rather gloomy view of the expedition. Under his command were 6 carriers, 2 battleships, 2 heavy cruisers, 1 light cruiser, 9 destroyers and 3 scouting submarines. There were also 9 tankers whose vital function was to refuel those ships (the majority) with insufficient capacity to make the long ocean voyage on their own. Other submarines had gone on ahead, with orders to surround Oahu and sink any American ships that left the harbour during or after the attack. Five of the subs were fitted with a new and secret weapon: midget submarines. These little two-man craft had only a limited range, and had to be carried close to Pearl Harbor. It was hoped that, once there, they would be able to sneak into the harbour itself and use their torpedoes with devastating effect on the unsuspecting American ships; if the torpedo-bombers failed, the midgets might even make the difference between the success and failure of the entire operation. Genda and other air experts were irritated by this, and predicted darkly that the presence of submarines in US waters would merely add to the risk of detection before the Japanese could launch their attack.

In all other respects, the Japanese did everything they could to conceal their intentions and achieve surprise. Elaborate measures were taken to persuade American intelligence that Japanese ships and planes were still in home waters: fresh aircraft were brought into Kyushu to maintain the flight patterns of the Pearl-Harbor-bound flyers, and fake "messages" were broadcast to give the illusion that planes and ships were in contact in Japanese waters.

Across the Pacific

The problem of bringing a warlike armada across 3,000 miles of a busy ocean was tackled with a daring which was characteristic of the entire operation. The task force would take the rarely used northern route, away from the busiest shipping lanes; that was why Hitokappu Bay provided an ideal rendezvous. The risk involved was considerable, for the weather in this part of the Pacific could be atrocious. Heavy seas might make refuelling impossible, forcing most of the Japanese ships to go back; and in combination with fog they might prevent the planes from taking off, or make it impossible for them to find the task force when their mission was accomplished. But the risks were outweighed by the strong probability of making the voyage without sighting another vessel; and the thorough Japanese had even checked this a few weeks earlier by sending a liner by the same route on an apparently harmless trip to Honolulu. Intelligence officers on the liner also confirmed what Japanese agents on Oahu had already reported – that American air patrols were at their thinnest north of the island, and did not extend beyond a 200-mile range. If the task force approached from the north, and the planes were launched when it was more than 200 miles from Oahu, the Americans might never find out where it was.

Radio silence was observed throughout the voyage: the task force could receive messages but none were to be sent out, since even one transmission might give away the ships' position. On board, there was great activity. A constant alert was maintained, and the airmen – now informed that their objective was the US Pacific Fleet – trained and studied hard. If Japanese intelligence was correct, they would find the Americans in Pearl Harbor; but they had to be ready for any contingency. The most favourable of these was that they would come upon the Americans in their deep-water anchorage, Lahaina, where any ships that were sunk would never be salvaged. The least favourable possibilities were that the American fleet would be found at sea and on the alert – or that the Japanese would not be able to locate them at all.

For the Japanese, with their keen sense of shame, this would have been a terrible blow. The Japanese warrior

13

Photograph taken aboard one of the aircraft carriers from which the attack on Pearl Harbor was launched. The Japanese captioned the photograph: "The moment at which the Hawaii surprise attack force is about to take off from the carrier . . . . On the faces of those who go forth to conquer and those who send them off there floats only that beautiful smile which transcends death . . ."

General Hideki Tojo, Prime Minister of Japan, announces to the Japanese people that the nation is at war with the USA. As one of those chiefly responsible for the attack on Pearl Harbor and other acts of aggression, Tojo was put on trial after the defeat of Japan and hanged as a war criminal.

approached battle in an exalted state of mind that seemed to leave him indifferent to death. This attitude was apparent in important aspects of their planning. For example, one of Genda's worries was that the American battleships might be protected by torpedo netting, although Japanese agents on Oahu thought that this was not the case. The flyers agreed on their own solution: if the nets were in place they would simply crash their aircraft through them, although this meant certain death. And they also agreed that any pilot who became lost on his way back after the attack would not break radio silence, but would plunge silently into the sea when his plane ran out of fuel.

Luck was with the Japanese all the way. No foreign vessels were sighted, and refuelling provided them with few problems. However, after almost two weeks at sea it was still possible that the operation would be called off if negotiations between Japan and the United States succeeded. Finally, on 2nd December, the task force, along with the rest of the Combined Fleet, received a radio message from Admiral Yamamoto: "Climb Mount Niitaka!"

Japan was going to war, and the date for the attack now became known. It was 8th December – or at Pearl Harbor, which lay in a different time zone on the other side of the International Date Line, 7th December, 1941.

Tora! Tora! Tora!

The take-off

In the early-morning darkness of 7th December, 1941, the Japanese task force came down from the north, plunging through heavy seas at a rate of 24 knots. A single light cruiser, backed by four destroyers, scouted ahead. At a distance followed the two battleships, each with a heavy cruiser riding escort. Behind this powerful spearhead, in two columns, came the carriers with their vital cargo of planes and flyers, protected on their flanks and rear by the most modern destroyers in the fleet.

At about 5:00 a.m. the flyers began to dress, then breakfasted and assembled in a state of high emotion for their final briefings. Most of them had left letters for their families in case they failed to return, putting in clippings from their fingernails and hair according to the Japanese custom. At the end of the briefing they drank a toast in *sake* and went into action. Before entering the cockpit, each pilot – like the Japanese warrior of old – tied round his head a scarf carrying the Japanese word *hissho:* "Certain Victory".

In the meantime, at 5:30, two seaplanes had been sent ahead to reconnoitre Pearl Harbor and Lahaina anchorage. There was an element of risk involved, since, though flying high, the Japanese planes might have been spotted, alerting the Americans. Furthermore, they would have to break radio silence in order to pass their information to the airborne strike force. But the Japanese judged the risk worth taking in return for up-to-the-minute information which might make all the difference between success and failure.

At 5:50 the carriers turned east into the wind, ready for the launch. Conditions were far from ideal, with the ships pitching about and sheets of spray driving across the flight decks. Any ordinary operation would have been put off until there was some improvement in the weather, but no margin for delay or error existed in Japan's carefully scheduled war planning. The situation was particularly hazardous for the first planes to take off, since the crowded decks left them with only a short run before they became airborne.

When the very first Zero roared away from the pitching bow of the flagship *Akagi*, it hung dangerously low over the

Commander Mitsuo Fuchida, who led the first-wave assault on Pearl Harbor.

waves for a moment, then climbed to safety while the men on the carrier cheered with relief. In the event, only one of the 185 first-strike planes crashed on take-off, while another developed engine trouble and had to be grounded. Under trying conditions the Japanese had put 183 aircraft into the sky within the space of a few minutes, triumphantly proving the value of the intensive training their pilots had undergone.

By about 6:20 a.m. 40 torpedo-planes, 49 bombers, 51 dive-bombers and 41 Zero fighters were in the air and on their way. While this first wave, led by Commander Mitsuo Fuchida, headed for Oahu, plane handlers on the carriers began working at top speed to bring up the machines that would form the second wave.

Missed opportunities

Luck was with the Japanese all the way. Even on the morning of the attack, several things happened that might have alarmed and alerted the American authorities on Oahu; but in every case the information that resulted was either not received or misinterpreted.

The first "warning" came at 3:50 a.m., when most of the Japanese flyers were still asleep on the carriers of the task force. By that time, the Japanese midget submarines were already lurking outside Pearl Harbor, on the lookout for opportunities to slip past the protective netting into the harbour itself. At 3:50 the deck officer of the *Condor*, an

A critical moment for the attackers: planes about to take off from one of the Japanese carriers. Heavy seas made the operation a hazardous one.

American minesweeper out on a routine patrol, sighted a periscope. The *Condor* signalled a destroyer, the *Ward*, which spent two hours searching the area but failed to confirm the sighting. Neither the *Condor* nor the *Ward* reported the incident – understandably enough, for mistaken sightings were common enough on night duty at sea, and no sensible officer wanted to be responsible for a baseless alarm.

At some point, while the harbour entrance was open for *Condor* to come in, one of the midget submarines crept through before the protective netting was dropped back into place. Another of the midgets was less fortunate. At 6:30 a US supply ship, the *Antares*, was towing a barge towards Pearl Harbor when her skipper noticed something that looked like a conning tower of unfamiliar design, about a mile away in the early dawn light. He reported it to the *Ward*, which rapidly went into action. The destroyer bore down on the Japanese submarine, hit it on the waterline and, after it submerged, finished it off with depth charges.

Ward's commander reported the action at 6:53, and within a few minutes a navy flying boat also claimed to have depth-charged and destroyed a submerged submarine – again, not far from the entrance to Pearl Harbor. The submarines had, after all, proved to be the weakest element in Yamamoto's planning, giving advanced warning of Japan's hostile intentions. But although these incidents were discussed at top level, the naval Commander-in-Chief, Admiral Kimmel, believed that they too might be false alarms, and decided to take no action until the sinkings could be confirmed. There was no general alert, and Kimmel saw no reason to warn the army. He had always expected Japanese submarine activity around Hawaii in the event of war, and probably felt that he could afford to be cautious in evaluating the situation, since the bulk of the fleet was safe in port. It never occurred to him that the submarines might be the advance guard of an air attack – or that minutes might be of vital importance to the survival of the fleet.

A last chance to oppose Fuchida's planes occurred just after 7:00, as the Opana Mobile Radar Station was closing down. The word "radar" stands for "radio detecting and ranging", and describes a system for detecting the approach of distant objects. When high-frequency radio pulses are sent out by a transmitter, any approaching object reflects the signal, and this shows up as a "blip" on a screen (oscilloscope). By December 1941 radar had already shown its value during the Battle of Britain, when it enabled the

Royal Air Force to intercept raiders during the German "Blitz". But the radar system on Oahu was rudimentary – used for training rather than defence – and only functioned from 4 until 7 in the morning. The Opana Station operated at the northernmost point of the island, and would have closed down more promptly if the breakfast truck had arrived on time. As it was, the two-man unit, Privates Lockard and Elliott, stared with surprise at the large cluster of blips that appeared on the screen, and first of all checked that their equipment was working properly. Then they called the Information Center 30 miles away and reported. The officer they spoke to was reassuring; he knew that a flight of B-17s ("Flying Fortress" bombers) was due to arrive from California, and assumed that these had caused the blips. This was secret information which he couldn't pass on to Lockard and Elliott, so he just said "Well, don't worry about it."

Charge!

In the air, the first wave under Fuchida was nearing Oahu, flying at altitudes from 3,000 to 4,300 metres above a thick layer of cloud that effectively hid it from observation. In the meantime the two seaplanes had made their reconnaissance without being detected, and at 7:35 they reported from Pearl Harbor and Lahaina anchorage. The fleet was in the harbour, and everything seemed normal. On the negative side, the anchorage was deserted, which ended Japanese hopes of sinking the American ships in deep water, where they could not possibly be salvaged; and there was no sign of the three US carriers. All the same, the news was good: the bulk of the Pacific Fleet had been located at Pearl Harbor and seemed to have no inkling that an attack was imminent.

At about the same time, Fuchida spotted the northern tip of Oahu through a break in the clouds. The Japanese planes hastily took up their attacking formation, most of them banking and following a course along the west side of the island before swinging round and homing in on their targets from the west and south. Then Fuchida fired a smoke flare from his rocket pistol – the "Black Dragon" signal, indicating that, since the enemy had been taken by surprise, the torpedo-planes should go straight into the attack against the American battleships.

Few large-scale military operations go completely smoothly, and the attack on Pearl Harbor was no exception.

The leader of one group of planes failed to see the flare, and Fuchida repeated the signal by firing again. But this only brought about a more serious mistake. The leader of the dive-bombers believed that this was an alternative, two-flare signal, indicating that the Americans were on the alert; in that case, the dive-bombers and bombers were to go in first, drawing the American fire upwards, so that the low-flying torpedo-men would have a chance to approach their targets. With the dive-bombers already on their way, Fuchida realized with alarm that the attack would not take place as planned.

All of this happened very quickly; a matter of seconds, not minutes, would decide whether the Japanese could strike home before the Americans manned their guns or took to the air. Fuchida did not hesitate. At 7:49 he ordered his wireless operator to tap out a signal to all pilots: TO TO TO, which stood for *totsugekiseyo* – charge!

Four minutes later it was already obvious that the mistakes over the order of attack would not affect the outcome: peaceful Sunday-morning Pearl Harbor lay at the mercy of the Japanese flyers. The exultant Fuchida now sent out the famous TORA! TORA! TORA! message. It meant TIGER! TIGER! TIGER!, and signified that complete surprise had been achieved. The signal was received by Nagumo aboard the task force flagship, *Akagi*, and by Yamamoto on the *Nagato* in the Inland Sea, three thousand miles away. Yamamoto, that inveterate gambler, is said to have been playing *shogi* (a chess-like game) when the news arrived – and, like any good gambler, to have maintained his poker face. The signal vindicated his judgement; although sent when the attack had hardly begun, it was in effect a victory signal.

Impact

Oahu was just as unsuspectingly quiet and sleepy as appearances suggested. On this laziest morning of the week, the only sounds to be heard were church bells ringing and a military band playing somewhere. A few navy men were on duty, carrying out routine tasks, and some others were at breakfast; many more were still fast asleep after enjoying their Saturday night "liberty" (shore leave). The fleet was in port and, as Japanese intelligence had foretold, on Battleship Row the mighty US battleships lay close together, double-berthed on the eastern side of Ford Island.

Although this was what he had been led to expect, Fuchida could not help marvelling at American carelessness in putting their ships so close together, so that they made a large, easy target. Not one of them was ready to get under way, for none of their stacks was smoking. Only three planes were airborne, on a routine patrol. Thoughts of an attack were so far from the Americans' minds that many of the ships' below-deck hatches – potential life-savers if promptly closed during an emergency – were firmly clipped back to allow more air into the stuffy interiors.

When the first bomb exploded, Rear-Admiral Furlong on the minelayer *Oglala* believed that it had been dropped from an American aircraft by accident – until he saw the red Rising Sun symbol on the plane's wing. Dozens of Americans reacted in much the same way. Officers at the Ford Island command centre made angry comments about dangerous flying by a plane they assumed was one of their own, until a bomb hit one of their hangars. Then they hastily sent out the first of the famous AIR RAID PEARL HARBOR radio messages.

While Japanese bombers hit the military airfields on Oahu, the Zeros looked out for American planes in the air; finding none, they began strafing enemy installations on the ground. Over the harbour, the torpedo-men were annoyed to see the dive-bombers darting in front of them and snatching the privilege of making the first strike against the American fleet. But their mood soon became exultant. The Japanese agents at Honolulu were proved right: there *were* no anti-torpedo nets guarding the battleships, so suicide attacks would not be necessary. And the modified torpedoes *did* make way through the shallow waters of the harbour.

As bombs rained down and explosions rocked their ships, a good many American service personnel grasped the situation quickly and acted, although others remained in shock for the first few minutes. Even the sharpest operated at a disadvantage, manning guns on lurching vessels that had already been hit, or even finding themselves without ammunition, so that they were compelled to waste precious time breaking open stores.

Minutes – even moments – were of critical importance, since everything was happening incredibly quickly. The sky filled with anti-aircraft fire as the American crews went into action, but down in the harbour tell-tale waterspouts erupted beside one American ship after another, signifying that Japanese torpedoes had found their targets. By 8 o'clock in

Oahu.

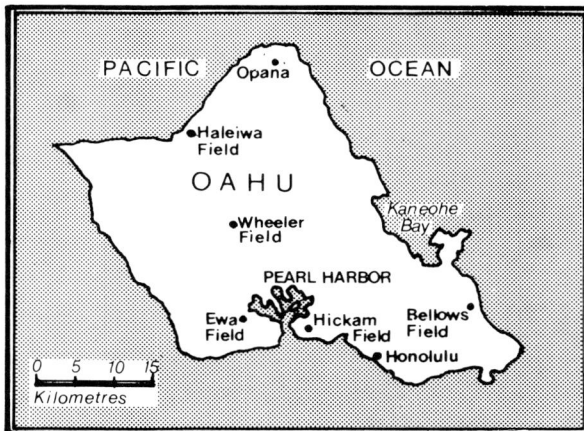

Pearl Harbor.

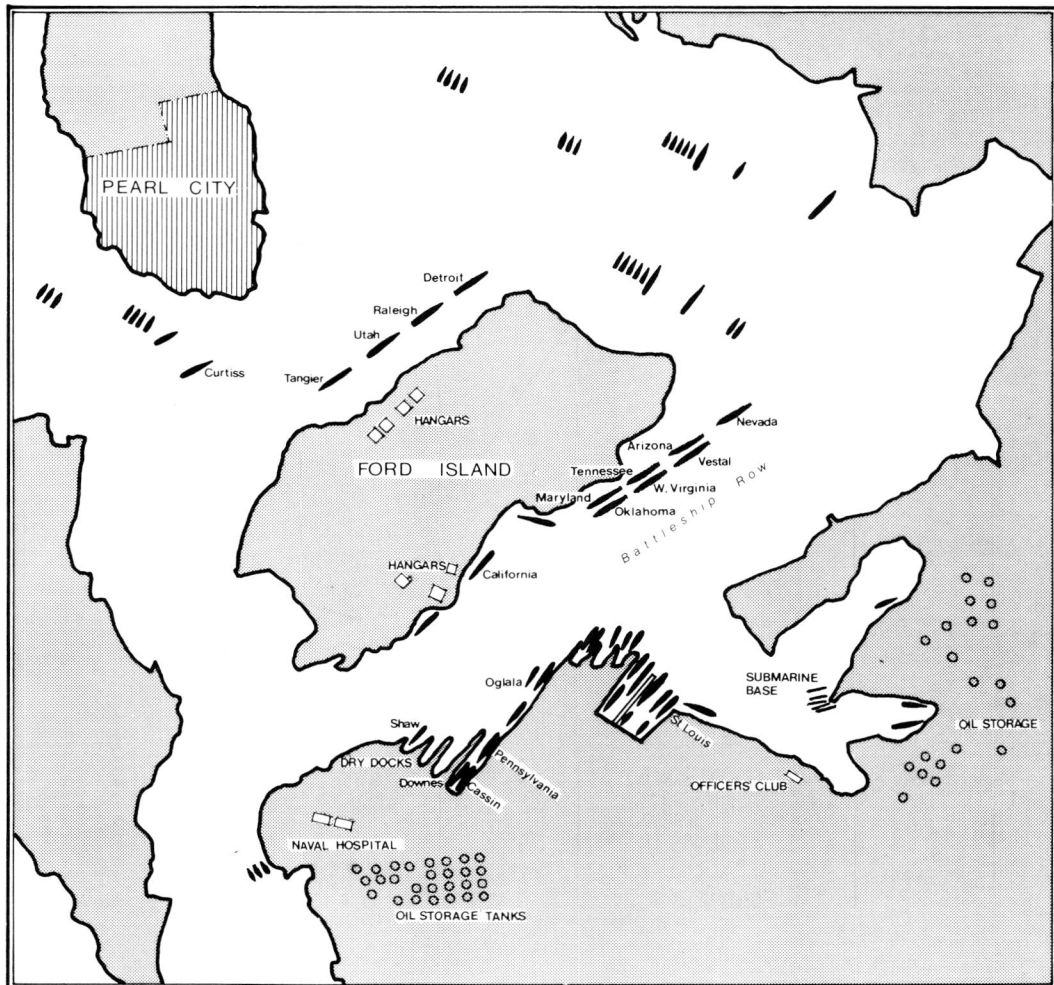

Japanese photograph of
Pearl Harbor, taken during
the attack. Torpedo tracks
and shock waves from
explosions can be seen in
the water to the left of the
line of US battleships.

the morning the Japanese had already inflicted massive damage on the fleet. Despite intensive training in ship recognition, they wasted two of their torpedoes on the *Utah*, which was only a target ship, but they sank one light cruiser, crippled another, and were spectacularly successful against the greatest prizes in the harbour – the battleships.

Japanese photograph of Pearl Harbor, taken during the attack. Torpedo tracks and shock waves from explosions can be seen in the water to the left of the line of US battleships.

Stricken giants

There were eight battleships in Pearl Harbor on Sunday, 7th December. One, *Pennsylvania*, was not in open water at all, but being worked on in dry dock; the rest were berthed on Battleship Row, facing south towards the harbour mouth. Furthest south, moored below a tanker and therefore at some distance from the others, lay the *California*. Then came three pairs of double-berthed vessels: *Maryland* inshore of *Oklahoma; Tennessee* inshore of *West Virginia*; and *Arizona* inshore of *Vestal*, which was not a battlewaggon but a repair ship. Furthest north, on its own at the end of the row, lay the battleship *Nevada*.

The *Oklahoma* and *West Virginia*, on the outside of their respective pairs, were prime targets, and Japanese torpedoes crashed into their flanks during the opening minutes of the attack; the *Arizona* was also hit by a missile that passed right under the repair ship on its outboard side. But these massive giants of steel were not easily destroyed, and the effect was not instantly apparent as one plane after another swept down low over the harbour and loosed a torpedo at one of the battlewaggons. Photographs taken from Japanese planes show the white trails left behind by these lethal "fish" (as servicemen called them) streaking through the water.

Under this battering, both the *West Virginia* and the *Oklahoma* began to list to port (the left-hand side of a ship – in this case, the side exposed to torpedo attack) as thousands of tons of water poured through the huge holes blasted out by Japanese missiles. The *West Virginia* had received early warning of the attack, and most of her crew were able to escape in time. Prompt action also saved her from the worst: in spite of the chaos, the gunnery officer was able to go below and organize counter-flooding. This involved opening the seacocks on the starboard side of the ship, so that the water also flowed in on that side; as a result, the *West Virginia* was not capsized by a weight of water concentrated on one side, but remained upright as she sank into the muddy floor of the harbour.

The crew of the *Oklahoma* was less alert, or perhaps just less lucky. Even as the klaxons sounded the call to battle stations, the first torpedo struck home. The battlewaggon began to list, and would-be defenders found their guns inadequately prepared and ammunition locked away. There were more explosions, and as water flooded from compartment to compartment (the *Oklahoma* was one of the vessels whose hatches were clipped back) the order was given to abandon ship. Hundreds of desperate men struggled to make their way to starboard and climb over the side as the ship slowly rolled over; then, when it had completely capsized, they crawled over on to the hull while Japanese machine-guns sprayed them with bullets. Below them were 400 sailors still trapped inside the *Oklahoma* – a horrific real-life version of a "disaster movie" situation.

Almost immediately afterwards, the *Arizona* was destroyed in an even more spectacular fashion. By this time the high-level bombers commanded by Fuchida himself were taking part in the attack. Several of them scored hits on the *Arizona*, but – as is often the case in the confusion of battle – it is not clear who released the fatal bomb, or even exactly where it landed; according to one story it actually went straight down the *Arizona's* stack (funnel). In any event, the

The USS Arizona, *on fire and enveloped in smoke after a Japanese bomb caused her powder magazines to explode. Over a thousand men on board were killed.*

bomb ignited the forward powder magazines, flames burst out of the guns of no. 2 turret, and there was a terrifying, ear-splitting explosion; it sent out shock waves that flung Fuchida's craft about as if it were a toy plane, and actually snuffed out the fires raging on the *Vestal* alongside the dying battleship. The other American vessels were showered with fragments of equipment and human bodies. The front part of the *Arizona* was engulfed in flames, there were more explosions, and a column of dark red smoke rose high over Pearl Harbor. Those who were not killed swam or sailed to safety around pools of flaming oil, but the death toll eventually rose to well over a thousand men out of the ship's complement of 1400. Among the dead were the ship's captain and Rear Admiral Kidd, commander of the First Battleship Division. Though no more than an abandoned, blazing hulk, *Arizona* continued to be bombed by the Japanese in their determination to put it beyond all hope of salvage.

The inshore battleships, protected against the torpedoes by the unlucky *West Virginia* and *Oklahoma*, escaped with relatively light damage. The *Tennessee* was struck by two bombs, but they hit nothing vital; the fires on her deck looked bad but were in fact superficial, caused by flaming debris from the *Arizona*. *Maryland* was even luckier. Fuchida himself dropped four bombs on her, and was delighted to record two hits; but as it turned out they did no serious damage.

Nevada, the tail-ender on Battleship Row, gave a particularly good account of herself. Her gun-crews got into position before she came under heavy attack, and the machine-gunners brought down two Japanese torpedo-planes. However, the second pilot managed to release his torpedo before crashing; it struck the *Nevada's* bows, tearing a 10 metres-wide hole in her port side. The flooded compartments were shut off, and although the ship took on a list, counter-flooding kept her afloat and even capable of getting under way.

The *California* was the last battleship to be hit – at 8:05, when her guns were already in action. But the two "fish" that bit into her had an immediate effect. Water poured into her port side, below the bridge, and through manholes left open for an imminent inspection; the fuel system was swamped and the ship's power supply failed. The *California* began to list, and although prompt counter-flooding saved her from the fate of the *Oklahoma*, the stern was set ablaze by burning oil. *California*, too, settled steadily into the mud.

The crew of the battleship California abandon ship as the stricken vessel sinks into the harbour mud. To the right can be seen the hull of the capsized Oklahoma.

Blasting the air bases

While groups of Japanese planes attacked the Pacific Fleet, dive-bombers swooped on other harbour installations. A prime target was the air base in the middle of Pearl Harbor itself, on Ford Island. Its hangars and flying-boat ramps were quickly shattered by bombs; one by one the planes, caught on the ground, blazed up as they were strafed by Japanese incendiary bullets. Servicemen, and later the fire service, struggled to control the flames, but with only limited success: surrounded by the waters of the harbour, they were nevertheless unable to make good use of their equipment because the *Arizona* had sunk on to the water mains.

Desperate calls from Pearl Harbor to the outlying air bases on Oahu achieved nothing, since these were also in trouble. Indeed, a great part of the Japanese effort was directed at the US airfields. The success of the attack on the fleet depended on maintaining mastery of the air, and so preventing American planes from interfering with the bombers; and it was equally important to nip in the bud any possible counter-strike against the Japanese naval task force.

The Japanese flyers were surprised and elated to meet so little resistance; one said later that the attack was more like a practice run than real combat. The Japanese were unopposed in the air, and their very light casualties were mainly the result of machine-gun or small-arms hits, scored on planes that screamed over the airfields at rooftop height to inflict maximum damage.

The most important bases were the two US Army fields, Wheeler and Hickam. Wheeler Field, north of Pearl Harbor, was utterly unprepared, although its complement of 80-odd aircraft included 50 of the most up-to-date American fighter planes. The Army command on Oahu had not worried much about an attack from the air, but instead concentrated on the possibility of sabotage by the island's large Japanese population. As a result, the planes at Wheeler Field were concentrated on the open "apron" at the base; row upon row of them stood with wingtips almost touching, all in one place where they could be efficiently guarded against saboteurs – and presented a sitting target for airborne attackers. At 7:56 Japanese dive-bombers screamed down on the field, blasting hangars and other installations; hundreds of sleeping servicemen were killed when the barracks were hit. And as the Japanese bombers and fighters returned again and again to shoot up the US aircraft on the ground, their task was made easier by the close-packing, which often caused one blazing plane to ignite its neighbour.

Conditions at Hickam Field, south-east of Pearl Harbor, were equally nightmarish, and the situation was further complicated by the appearance of a flight of American B-17s, ready to land. These were the planes whose expected arrival had earlier led to the tragic blunder over the radar report. They were mighty bombers – the "Flying Fortresses" later to be famous in the Second World War – but on this occasion they were defenceless, arriving unarmed and in need of refuelling on a long trip from California to the Philippines. Although the Zeros closed in on them, they were surprisingly successful at taking evasive action, scattering and managing to land – in some cases full of machine-gun holes – at various places on the island. Another unsuspecting flight of US planes was less fortunate: as they flew into Ford Island, Zeros shot down four of them and, in the smoke and confusion, American anti-aircraft fire brought down another.

Other American airfields suffered almost as badly as Wheeler and Hickam. At Ewa Field, the marine air base to the west of Pearl Harbor, Zeros destroyed an impressive number of planes on the ground; similarly, at Kaneohe, the naval air base on the eastern coast of the island, they shot up the US flying boats as they floated in the harbour or lay parked on the ramp. In both places, dive-bombers then descended and wrecked the permanent fixtures. All in all, the attack on the airfields had been as great a surprise, and as great a success, as the attack on the Pacific Fleet.

Interlude: grim farce

From the Japanese point of view, only the participation of the submarines was a failure – although they did not realize this at the time, since they mistakenly credited one of the midgets with the sinking of the *Arizona*. In reality, the submarines had proved a liability, achieving nothing while almost giving away the presence of the task force. Not one of the midgets survived (a fact that makes it difficult to describe their movements with any confidence) and only one member of the crews lived to tell his tale. Given the Japanese sense of honour, Ensign Sakamaki might have preferred death to his actual fate. His craft was malfunctioning, and for hours he and his crewman struggled to approach the harbour mouth. They were still struggling when the attack on Pearl Harbor began, having been carried – not once but three times – on to a coral reef. About half an hour after the start of the attack an American destroyer, the *Helm*, managed to escape the Japanese onslaught through the harbour mouth, and, spotting the sub, fired on it. The shot, or the submarine's impact against the coral reef, did further damage, but Sakamaki managed to submerge and escape. The craft remained out of control, and for the rest of the day could not be manoeuvred into the harbour. The exhausted Japanese eventually realized that they must abandon ship. The crewman drowned, but the unlucky Sakamaki was washed up, unconscious, on the east coast beach of Oahu. Instead of having a glorious death, he became the Second World War's first Japanese prisoner of war.

The "lull"

About half an hour after it had begun, the Japanese attack began to lessen in intensity and finally petered out. The jubilant flyers winged their way back to the task force with empty bomb racks and depleted supplies of ammunition.

Behind them they left an appalling scene of multi-coloured, billowing smoke, fierce flames, death, destruction and confusion. On land, alarm bells rang and vehicles dashed about, transporting the injured or taking officers to their posts. In the harbour itself, large numbers of small craft darted round the pools of blazing oil and past damaged and capsized vessels, rescuing men from the water. Hundreds of casualties with terrible burns or other wounds were taken to improvised hospital quarters, where the medical staff coped as best they could by using quantities of pain-killing morphine to lessen the victims' sufferings. And, dominating the entire harbour, a several-thousand-foot-high pall of smoke hung in the air, fed by a column swirling up from the ruined carcase of the *Arizona*.

But despite the apparent chaos, the Americans began to get ready for the renewed attack which they were rightly expecting. Everywhere men hurried to take up their duties (at Pearl Harbor some were so impatient that they swam out to their ships rather than wait for transport); supplies of ammunition were obtained and guns manned; and at the Oahu air bases, efforts were made to clear runways of debris and blazing pools of fuel, in the hope of putting some planes into the air.

But there was hardly time to do very much: twenty minutes or so after the end of the first attack, the second wave arrived – 132 high-level bombers and dive-bombers, led by Lieutenant-Commander Shigekazu Shimazaki and escorted by 35 Zero fighters.

The second strike

Since the Japanese could no longer rely on the element of surprise, it would have been suicidal to use low-flying torpedo-bombers to try to finish off the American fleet in the harbour. This became the job of the dive-bombers, whose swift, angled descent from on high made them much harder to hit, even by anti-aircraft crews at the ready.

Moments before the new onslaught began, another submarine drama was played out. In the channel on the eastern side of Ford Island, the destroyer *Monaghan* received a signal from the seaplane tender *Curtiss*, which claimed to have spotted a submarine; the Americans were amazed, since they had not believed that the harbour waters were deep enough for such a vessel to operate in. The enemy vessel was in fact one of the midget submarines, and it was also the only one to successfully enter Pearl Harbor. The *Monaghan* and other ships opened fire on the sub, which began to surface. It let off a torpedo at the *Curtiss*, but missed. The *Monaghan* bore down at full speed, rammed the midget and made certain of a kill by dropping two depth charges. The submarine and its occupants were destroyed, but the *Monaghan* also suffered: speeding away from the impact of the depth charges (which might have damaged it in the shallow waters of the harbour), the destroyer crashed into a barge – an incident that would have seemed like slapstick in different circumstances. However, despite the heavy bombing that was now going on, the *Monaghan* made its way to safety through the harbour mouth.

Attack on the Nevada

The *Nevada* was also on the move, despite the gaping hole in her side. Unlike the other US battleships, she had been partly under steam when the attack began, and while the second onslaught was in progress she began to move away from the blazing oil slicks that threatened her. As the *Nevada* headed south, past the still-burning hulk of the *Arizona* and the upturned hull of the *Oklahoma*, the Japanese planes swarmed in on her. As a battleship she was a prime target; and because she was moving she was relatively easy to pick out through the clouds of smoke and anti-aircraft fire that filled the sky, making accurate bombing difficult and hazardous. For twenty minutes the bombers tried to sink the *Nevada*, hoping to

◁ *After the attack. These vessels were stranded and helpless in dry dock when the Japanese struck. In front, the destroyers Downes and Cassin; behind, the battleship Pennsylvania, which by sheer luck escaped really serious damage.*

block the channel and so immobilize the entire fleet at Pearl Harbor; but, though hit several times and in appearance reduced to a wreck, the ship was successfully grounded on the eastern side of the harbour.

Although operating under greater difficulties than the first wave, Shimazaki's men had some notable successes. They located the dry docks and scored direct hits on the battleship *Pennsylvania*; and the American cruisers and destroyers also suffered. The most spectacular moments occurred when a direct hit in the forward magazine of the destroyer *Shaw* blew up the ship, followed shortly afterwards by the destruction of two more destroyers, the *Cassin* and the *Downes*, whose torpedoes and magazines were ignited by burning fuel-oil or enemy bombs. Although some destroyers managed to slip away, it seemed evident by the end of the Japanese attack that the US Pacific Fleet had been crippled.

Meanwhile, the high-level bombers and fighters were finishing off the American planes and air bases. The Zeros went in first and dealt with any opposition in the air; then the bombers did their work. When the dive-bombers' racks were empty, they too flew over the airfields, joining in the strafing. A few American planes did get into action from two small fields, Bellows and Haleiwa, that had not been damaged in the first attack; and they acquitted themselves well despite the fact that the Japanese enjoyed overwhelming superiority in numbers and possessed faster and more manoeuvrable fighters. But they could do little to check the continuing destruction.

It was still not 10 o'clock in the morning when the attack ended and the Japanese planes disappeared into the distance. There was a last moment of action when the cruiser *St Louis* made her way through the harbour entrance and narrowly avoided being hit by two torpedoes dispatched by a midget submarine. The *St Louis* fired at the sub, which submerged. But it was evidently hit, since it was never seen again. Ironically, the last shots fired during Japan's surprise attack on Pearl Harbor – like the first shots – came from American guns.

The same day

Flight and pursuit

The last Japanese plane to leave the skies over Pearl Harbor was Commander Mitsuo Fuchida's bomber. As the commander of the air operation, Fuchida had been present throughout, despite the fact that his fuselage had taken serious punishment during the first attack. In the closing minutes he continued to take photographs of the action and, peering through the clouds of smoke, tried to make a final assessment of the injuries sustained by the enemy. "I counted four battleships definitely sunk and three severely damaged, and extensive damage had also been inflicted on other types of ships. The seaplane base at Ford Island was all in flames, as were the airfields, especially Wheeler Field."

In Fuchida's mind, a third attack was still a possibility, since he realized that the huge fuel stores and other targets on Oahu had not yet been destroyed. But when he returned to the task force flagship, his superiors rejected the idea. Genda remained true to his belief in the vital role of carriers in Pacific warfare; therefore he dismissed another attack as too risky, but favoured remaining in the area to locate and destroy the missing American flattops. As commander of the task force, Nagumo overruled them both. He had never been enthusiastic about the Pearl Harbor plan and, although he was overjoyed that it had worked so well, was reluctant to push his luck any further. The task force had accomplished its main objective: the US fleet would not be capable of interfering with Japan's "Southern Operation" in Asia, and Yamamoto would have his six months in which to "run wild". Nagumo decided to bring his ships and planes home. In the Inland Sea, Yamamoto, the man who had conceived of the plan, refused to order Nagumo to take further action, believing that it was necessary to trust the judgement of the man on the spot, who knew all the circumstances. The Commander-in-Chief ordered his battleships to stand by to help the task force if the Americans went into action against it.

The Americans had every intention of doing so: they had two small task forces of their own at sea, including two of the carriers the Japanese had hoped to find in harbour. They were prepared to hit back at the Japanese force – if they could find it. For it was literally true that the Americans didn't know what had hit them. The Japanese might have descended from a few unescorted carriers, which ought to be promptly counter-attacked; but on the other hand their onslaught from the air might be only the prelude to a full-scale invasion. In this atmosphere of uncertainty, many Americans spent 7th December in fire-fighting, rescue and salvage operations. Others tried to calm the civilian population of Honolulu, who were distressed by the bombardment they had undergone – actually the result of American guns at Pearl Harbor overshooting their targets. The majority of service personnel were placed on full alert and made ready to face a seaborne invasion that never came.

However, despite heavy losses, the Americans managed to send up a handful of search planes an hour or so after the Japanese attack had ended. With only limited resources, they looked for the enemy task force in the most plausible direction – to the south, the direction from which Fuchida's men had hit Pearl Harbor. As a result of this wrong guess, the Japanese escaped undetected; and this was probably just as well, from an American point of view, since a carrier-based attack on the powerful Japanese task force would most likely have ended with the precious US flattops being sent to the bottom of the Pacific Ocean – just the outcome Genda had most ardently hoped for.

Japan triumphant

Even as matters stood, the cost to the USA was high. Eight battleships, three light cruisers, three destroyers and four other ships were sunk or badly damaged. Something like 180 planes were destroyed and 130 damaged. The final American death toll was 2,403, of whom all but 68 were servicemen; and well over a thousand Americans were more or less seriously wounded.

The blow was as devastating as the Japanese intended, and far less costly than they had anticipated. In particular, not a single surface ship was lost, although one large and five midget submarines failed to return. Only 29 planes were brought down over Oahu. A good many more were damaged by American fire, and rough seas caused some to crash-land on the carrier decks, from which they had to be tipped hastily into the water so that other aircraft could set down before their fuel was exhausted.

This was an astonishingly cheap price to pay for such a daring, large-scale operation; yet the attack on Pearl Harbor was only one element in a still greater, superbly coordinated scheme. Dozens of Japanese troop transports, crammed with soldiers and escorted by fighting ships and planes, were on the move over vast areas of the Pacific. The first shots in the "Southern Operation" were fired only minutes before the 7th December attack on Pearl Harbor. (However, in South-East Asia, which lies west of the International Date Line, it was already 8th December.) Within twenty-four hours the Japanese had invaded Thailand and two British colonies, Malaya (modern Malaysia) and Hong Kong. They also

Sailors leaping from the sinking Prince of Wales *after the Japanese attack on 10th December, 1941.*

launched air attacks against the US bases on the Pacific islands of Guam and Wake, and destroyed most of the US aircraft on the ground in a raid on the American-protected Philippine Islands.

Two days later, Japanese planes sank the British battleships *The Prince of Wales* and *The Repulse*, which were not provided with air cover. This confirmed that experts such as Genda were right in believing that naval warfare had changed: battleships were no longer queens of the ocean, unsinkable except by other battleships. The immediate result was that there was now nothing to hold up the Japanese invasions. The months that followed witnessed a string of victories that carried the Japanese Empire to the heights of its power and glory.

The "day of infamy"

Formal declarations of war by Britain and the United States followed less than twenty-four hours after the attack on Pearl Harbor. In Washington, D.C., at 12:30 p.m. on 8th December – 7:00 a.m. Hawaiian time – President Roosevelt entered the Capitol and addressed Congress. He began: "Yesterday, December 7th, 1941 – a date which will live in infamy – the United States was deliberately attacked by the naval and air forces of the Empire of Japan."

The "date which will live in infamy" became a famous phrase. At the end of his speech, the President asked Congress to declare war on Japan, and Congress voted overwhelmingly to do so.

War fever, 1940: Japanese troops, back from the fighting in China, are given a heroes' welcome.

THE INVESTIGATION

Why did Japan attack?

Japan and the colonial empires

In the early years of the twentieth century Japan's position in Asia was unique. Most Asian peoples were not self-governing, but belonged to colonies controlled by "white", non-Asian powers. Britain possessed the greatest of the Asian colonial empires, ruling India (which then comprised modern India, Pakistan and Bangladesh), Burma, Malaya, Hong Kong, Borneo and other territories. The French were masters of Indo-China (modern Vietnam, Cambodia and Laos) and the Dutch of the East Indies (modern Indonesia). The United States controlled the Philippines and various islands in the Pacific. Some Asian countries enjoyed independence in name, but were in reality under the indirect control of the colonial powers. This was true even of China, which despite her enormous size had remained weak and backward. Only Japan had kept her independence and also managed to build up a strong modern state that could stand comparison with the Euro-American powers.

A divinely favoured people

This situation encouraged the Japanese to believe that they were a people with a special destiny. Japan's past had already made this a plausible belief, since the Japanese lived under an emperor whose god-given authority had never in their entire history been seriously challenged. In Japanese legend the first emperor, Jimmu, had descended from the Plains of Heaven in 660 BC; and the emperors had ruled Japan in unbroken succession ever since. For long periods, real power was exercised by strong men or clans, but it was always done in the name of the emperor. So the Japanese never became disillusioned by changes in government, but thought of themselves as members of a divinely favoured order of things.

The divine wind

Divine favour was also shown by the fact that Japan had never been successfully invaded and occupied. At the most desperate moment, when a Mongol armada was poised to invade, it was wrecked by a typhoon (1281); the Japanese named this the *kamikaze*, or "divine wind", and it was to have a powerful effect on their thinking. A people under the direct protection of Heaven could dare much and overcome even the strongest enemy.

The Japanese way of life

The Japanese had a great gift for taking over other peoples' ideas and techniques, and then adapting them to their own purposes. In the early history of Japan, the borrowings – which even included the script in which the Japanese language was written – were mainly from the Chinese. But the Japanese were not slavish imitators; they made use of foreign ideas while maintaining their own culture. The Japanese way of life emphasized authority and obedience, and made a cult of the

The samurai was the knight of old Japan, famous for his swordsman's skills, fearlessness and loyalty to his lord. The image of the samurai remained potent between the world wars, and influenced Japanese behaviour during the Second World War.

warrior (the *samurai*, or knight), who was bound by a strict code of honour (*bushido*). A breach of the code, even accidental, constituted a personal disaster; like other instances of "loss of face" (humiliation), it left an honourable man no alternative but to commit ritual suicide (*hara-kiri*); and, in general, the Japanese warrior embraced death with a willingness – even fervour – that was rarely found in the West.

Japanese isolationism

When foreign ideas threatened to disturb Japanese life too thoroughly, Japan's rulers simply shut them out; foreigners were kept out of the country and Japanese were forbidden to go abroad on pain of death. From the seventeenth to the mid-nineteenth century Japan remained isolated from a world that was increasingly dominated by the great powers of Europe and the USA. Then, in 1853-54, the American Commodore Matthew Perry forced the Japanese – more or less at the point of a gun – to resume contact and trade with the West.

Modernization and empire

A Japanese military pilot during the First World War. As the picture suggests, the Japanese were quick to recognize the potential of air power. The territories Japan gained as a result of the war served as springboards for their campaigns in 1941-2.

Once more the Japanese showed how adaptable they could be. Within a generation or so, Japan had acquired factories and railways, founded a system of mass education, and set up a parliament along western lines. The army was modernized, and a new fleet of warships played an important part in Japan's first venture into international politics – a war against China (1894-95) in which the victorious Japanese replaced the Chinese as "protectors" of Korea and gained possession of the very large Chinese island of Formosa. Japan was now considered important enough to become an ally of the British Empire, which at that time (1902) seemed to be the greatest power in the East. Even so, Japan's victory over Russia in

1904-5 astonished the world, since few people had seriously believed that "orientals" could take on any European power and win. In 1910 Japan annexed Korea, and in 1914 she entered the First World War on the side of the Allies against Germany and Austria. As a result, the German-held groups of islands in the northern Pacific (the Carolines, Marshalls and Marianas) fell into Japanese hands. (As a glance at the map on pages 10-11 will show, these islands were ideally placed to become the forward posts for Japan's advance in the Pacific during the Second World War.) In April 1918, even before the end of the First World War, Japanese and British marines landed at Vladivostok in Siberia. This was part of a pattern of interventions in Russia by the great powers, designed to overthrow the Bolshevik (Communist) government established after the October Revolution of 1917; however, the Bolsheviks survived and the powers (including Japan) eventually withdrew.

The samurai tradition

All this indicates that Japan had become a successful and notably aggressive nation. But although modernized, she had not become western in outlook. Many of the great changes in Japanese society had been initiated by the Emperor or his advisers, so that the old authority, and the old values, carried over into modern Japan; the warrior, fanatically devoted to his Emperor and heedless of his own life, remained an ideal figure. However, before blaming Japanese militarism on the *samurai* tradition, it is as well to remember that much Japanese behaviour was not so very different from that of the western powers. They too had bullied and wrung concessions from backward China, had demanded "a place in the sun" (at the expense of other people) and had intrigued and fought for economic advantages, political influence and possessions. In many respects, Japan simply behaved as a late-comer, hurrying to grab her share of Asia's spoils.

Democracy on trial

The modernization of Japan occurred so quickly that the old values remained strong; but after a time they might well have given way to new forces that were also at work in the West – forces such as democracy, socialism, trade unionism, humanitarianism and internationalism, all of which were at odds with the militarist outlook. In the 1920s there were signs that this was happening. There were serious industrial disputes and bitter conflicts over who should have the right to vote; and, on the policy level, some Japanese governments were far more conciliatory towards China and Soviet Russia.

Economic difficulties

Then came the Great Depression, an international economic collapse that began in 1929 on Wall Street, the heart of the US financial system, and continued far into the 1930s. Japan was hit very hard; millions of people were impoverished, and foreign markets for Japanese goods shrank because buyers were ruined or were impelled by their governments to spend their money on home-produced goods. The situation was particularly serious because the Japanese population was soaring, thus increasing the general hardship and making the idea of overseas expansion very attractive.

Militarism triumphant

This caused a drastic change of mood within Japan. Nationalist feeling ran high, and the military became dominant in Japanese life. The government remained nominally civilian, but Japanese politicians generally held power only while they did what the armed forces wanted; in fact the most serious political disagreements tended to be those between the army and the navy, which sometimes had widely different ideas about how and where Japanese expansion should take place. Neither doubted that Japan *should* expand; and from 1931 the country was set on the

The Emperor Hirohito in about 1936. Although venerated by his subjects, the Emperor allowed his ministers and military men to decide Japan's destiny. He seems to have disliked the idea of war with the USA, but did little to discourage the Japanese militarists.

course of aggression that was to lead to Pearl Harbor. Possession of new territories was desirable because it would guarantee markets for Japanese goods and provide raw materials for Japanese industries. A programme of arms manufacture and shipbuilding also stimulated the economy and helped Japan to recover from the Depression, though this result could almost certainly have been achieved by public spending on peaceful projects.

"The China Incident"

Japanese troops occupy a Chinese village during the invasion of Manchuria in 1931. Japanese aggressions culminated in a full-scale invasion (1937) which the Japanese tried to dismiss as a trivial matter by labelling it "the China Incident". But the problems created by Chinese resistance were partly responsible for Japan's aggressions elsewhere, including Pearl Harbor.

The first victim was China. In 1931 the Japanese army used a minor incident as an excuse to take over the large northern Chinese province of Manchuria, which became "independent" under a puppet ruler "advised" by Japan. Racked by divisions between Nationalists, Communists and other groups, China was forced to agree, and found it hard to resist further Japanese demands; but when the Japanese

launched a full-scale invasion in July 1937, the Chinese did manage to unite against the aggressor. Although the Japanese advanced deep into the country there was no surrender, and the sheer vastness of China added to Japanese difficulties. They always referred to this war as "the China Incident", but their expectations of a quick victory were disappointed and their armies were obviously becoming bogged down. In 1939 they adopted a new strategy, seizing the seaports of China and aiming to break the stubborn Chinese by an economic blockade. However, there were still two routes through which the Chinese could get supplies – by rail from French Indo-China and along the British-controlled "Burma Road". This made a thrust into South-East Asia an attractive but very dangerous option for the Japanese: if successful, they could ensure victory in China by cutting the Burmese and Indo-Chinese lifelines while simultaneously seizing the tin, rubber, oil, tungsten, rice and other rich resources of the area. With the outbreak of the Second World War, the prospect was to become even more attractive and rather less dangerous.

The influence of fascism

Japan was not alone in turning to militarism. During the 1930s militarized states and open aggressions became so common that many people believed the "democratic age" was coming to an end. Fascist Italy, led by Mussolini, and Nazi Germany, under Adolf Hitler, successfully broke treaties and absorbed weaker states while democratic Britain and France made only feeble protests. Japan, Germany and Italy had many features in common, and were eventually to become allies in the Second World War. As well as their military-style societies (often given the general name "fascist"), they were fanatically hostile to Communism. As early as 1936 they signed the Anti-Comintern Pact, directed specifically against the Soviet Union. An invasion of the Soviet Far East was a scheme much favoured by the Japanese army, which twice tried to pull Japan into a new war by using small border incidents as excuses for aggression, just as it had done in Manchuria. But in July 1938, and again in May 1939, Japanese attacks across the Manchurian border met with such swift, harsh counters from Soviet forces that the Japanese hastily backed off.

The Second World War

The outbreak of the Second World War brought opportunities in a different direction. By the summer of 1940 Hitler's Germany had overrun most of Europe, including France and Holland; Britain remained free, but alone and at bay. With three of the colonial powers paralysed or preoccupied

Axis representatives celebrating the Tripartite Pact of September 1940, which strengthened the ties between Japan, Nazi Germany and Fascist Italy. Foreign Minister Matsuoka proposes a toast; on his right, bespectacled and bemedalled, stands General Tojo, who was to become Japan's war leader.

elsewhere, there were now few obstacles to Japanese expansion in South-East Asia. In June 1940, shortly after the German victory in France, the Japanese established a military mission in French Indo-China, and in September this was converted into a military occupation of the northern part of the country. China's Haiphong-Kunming lifeline was cut, and Japan had secured a valuable foothold in South-East Asia. Almost immediately afterwards Japan signed the Tripartite Pact, which bound Germany, Italy and Japan to fight together in the event of any new war breaking out.

The American presence In this situation, the United States was the only power with an Asian "military presence" that could hope to oppose

Japanese expansion; and that was why the Japanese eventually attacked at Pearl Harbor and tried to eliminate the US Pacific Fleet. In the 1930s the United States government had protested again and again about Japanese aggression in China, but many – perhaps most – Americans had no wish to get involved in other peoples' wars. This outlook, known as isolationism, put strict limits on the help President Roosevelt could give to China.

With the outbreak of war in Europe, Japanese-American relations grew steadily worse. Hitler's triumph on the continent of Europe prompted the Americans to start building a "two-ocean navy" that would make them safe and strong in both the Atlantic and the Pacific. Meanwhile, though there was no question of the United States entering the war, Roosevelt did everything he could to help Britain survive the German onslaught; American supplies flowed across the Atlantic, and the US Navy gave much covert help to the Royal Navy in its struggle against German submarines.

Embargoes against Japan

The "undeclared war" in the Atlantic made Roosevelt anxious to avoid, or at least to put off, a conflict in the East. To try to deter Japanese aggression, the Pacific Fleet was moved forward from the West Coast of the USA to Pearl Harbor. After the occupation of French Indo-China, the President began to forbid the export of certain goods to Japan; these embargoes eventually extended to all war materials, including iron and steel scrap and fuel – a heavy blow to a nation such as Japan, which had few mineral resources of her own. And, however remote the prospect of a settlement, the Americans were glad to keep talks with the Japanese going. The European war entered a critical phase after 22nd June, 1941, when Nazi Germany attacked the Soviet Union, and increasing American involvement with the Anglo-Soviet alliance made the maintenance of peace in the Pacific seem even more important.

Futile diplomacy

The Japanese were also prepared to talk, while getting ready to strike without warning if talk failed to produce results. With the United States openly sympathetic to the Allied (Anglo-Soviet) cause, and Japan bound by treaty to the Axis (Italian and German) powers, it is difficult to see how agreement could have been reached. Although diplomats on both sides spoke and wrote many thousands of words, the basic positions were these: Japan would promise to keep the peace if the United States would recognize her paramount

role in eastern Asia, leave her a free hand in China and lift the embargoes; while the United States insisted that Japan must give up her conquests *and* keep the peace – in which case, the American Secretary of State assured her envoys, "The United States would be glad to give Japan all she wants in the way of materials."

Japan's timetable for war Neither side had much faith in diplomacy, but they were in very different situations. The Americans were playing for

◁ *Franklin D. Roosevelt (left)
and Winston Churchill
meet in mid-Atlantic in
August 1941. Although
neutral, the United States
was deeply involved with
Britain's struggle against
Nazi Germany – a fact that
influenced US dealings with
Japan.*

time: the Japanese were running out of it. Delay could only strengthen the United States as her rearmament programme gathered momentum and she reinforced her defences in the Philippines; whereas Japan would soon begin to grow weaker. In particular, Japan's oil reserves were dwindling fast; if she waited until 1942 she would be unable to sustain a war for any reasonable length of time. This made the Southern Operation, and especially the conquest of the oil-rich Dutch East Indies, even more desirable. By mid-October the Japanese had a timetable prepared that would admit of no alteration: taking into consideration the weather, oil reserves and the possibility of an attack on Siberia the following spring, Japan would have to go to war early in December. In the event, the planners decided on 8th December, Japanese time (7th December, Hawaiian time). Talks went on until the last moment, and although the Pearl Harbor task force left Hitokappu Bay on 26th November, it remained possible that they might be recalled.

Instead, the attack on Pearl Harbor and the Southern Operation went ahead; Japan and the United States were at war. Then, on 10th December, Japan's German and Italian allies declared war on the United States, which was at last brought into the Second World War.

Why were the Americans taken by surprise?

Who was to blame?

Americans were shocked and angered by the news about Pearl Harbor. Their anger was directed against the Japanese, whose attack had the effect of uniting all sections of US opinion. But even as they made ready for war, the American public were asking how their forces could have been caught so completely off guard. To find out, the President ordered a formal inquiry; and the report of the Roberts Commission in February 1942 put most of the blame on the Navy and Army commanders on Oahu, Admiral Kimmel and General Short. There have been arguments about the justness of this verdict ever since, and many writers have disagreed with it, putting some or even all of the blame on the United States government.

Admiral Husband E. Kimmel, naval commander on Hawaii.

Lieutenant General Walter C. Short, commander of the US Army ground and air forces on Hawaii.

"The strongest fortress in the world"

There was certainly a case to answer. Both the government and the military leaders knew that Japan was an expansionist nation, and that the Japanese had little respect for treaties and a marked taste for surprise attacks. And, to all appearances, Pearl Harbor should have been the least vulnerable of American bases, since it had been widely advertised as impregnable – "the strongest fortress in the world", according to the Army Chief of Staff, General Marshall.

Military blunders The Americans' mistakes were most obvious on and around Oahu, revealing a complete failure to anticipate and prepare for a Japanese attack. The navy air patrols were inadequate, and no attempt was made to reinforce them by borrowing army planes. On the island, the Army and Navy were not on the alert on Sunday, 7th December, despite the fact that the fleet assembled in the harbour presented a large and invaluable target. It was fairly easy for the Japanese to be sure that the fleet would be in port at the moment they struck, since it followed a fixed routine – an elementary blunder at a time when war was imminent. There were no torpedo nets protecting the battleships. And on the island's airfields, US planes were in their hangars or packed wingtip-to-wingtip, as if to simplify the attackers' task. All of these were essentially failures on the part of the top-level commanders; but there were other, local failures which indicated that "Other Ranks" were equally oblivious of danger – the casual response to the radar report, the clipped-back flood doors, the ammunition and other equipment that was not to hand when it was needed.

Dereliction of duty? The simplest explanation is that Kimmel and Short were incompetent, or, worse, were guilty of "dereliction of duty". The Roberts Commission thought so, and its verdict ended the commanders' careers. But even if this were true, it would fail to explain why two men with excellent records should have got things so disastrously wrong: the "incompetence" is something that itself needs an explanation.

An obsession with sabotage And this explanation seems to be that neither Kimmel nor Short believed there was the slightest possibility of a Japanese air raid on Pearl Harbor. You do not waste time and resources in taking precautions against the impossible. As far as General Short was concerned, the main danger to the American bases came from sabotage. Reports from the European war suggested that Hitler's successes owed much to fascist sympathizers ("fifth columnists") working behind the Allied lines; the reports were exaggerated, but Short could not know that. Hawaii's very large population of Japanese immigrants seemed an obvious danger, and so the American planes were assembled and guarded against saboteurs instead of being dispersed to protect them against an air attack that was never likely to occur. His line of thought remained undisturbed even when Washington sent him a War Warning message on 27th November. Since it ended with an instruction to avoid alarming the civilian population, Short took what he believed to be the appropriate action, stepping up his training programme and intensifying anti-sabotage precautions.

Looking in the wrong direction

It was Short's job to defend the fleet when it was in port, but it evidently never struck him as requiring any special measures. Admiral Kimmel felt the same: the only threat he feared was enemy submarine activity in the waters beyond Pearl Harbor. Otherwise his planning was for offensive, not defensive, action: the fleet must be ready to move out and intervene somewhere further west when war came. When Kimmel received his 27th November War Warning, it must have reinforced his attitude, for attached to the warning was an intelligence report predicting that the Japanese were most likely to attack Thailand, the Philippines or Borneo. During the week that followed, Kimmel behaved quite logically from his own point of view, sending the carriers *Enterprise* and *Lexington* to deliver planes to Midway and Wake Island, US outposts much further west in the Pacific, where it seemed more likely that trouble would break out. Ironically, this saved them from almost certain destruction in Pearl Harbor when the Japanese attacked.

American over-confidence

In the final analysis, Kimmel and Short must take much of the blame for the disaster at Pearl Harbor. It is almost the first duty of military leaders to guard against surprise attacks; and a single War Warning, even if it is not as crisply worded as possible, should have been sufficient. But, if not excusable, the commanders' mistakes were understandable. Their belief in the invulnerability of Oahu was widely shared. Marshall pointed out that it had "a garrison of approximately 35,000 men, manning 127 fixed coast defense guns, 211 anti-aircraft weapons, and more than 3,000 artillery pieces and automatic weapons available for beach defense". And a Honolulu newspaper noted on 6th September that "A Japanese attack on Hawaii is regarded as the most unlikely thing in the world, with one chance in a million of being successful. Besides having more powerful defenses than any other post under the

American flag, it is protected by distance." Both comments assumed, quite wrongly, that the only form of attack contemplated by the Japanese would be an all-out assault with troop landings on the beaches; to that extent they suggest that the Americans had not fully appreciated the potential of carrier-borne aircraft in Pacific warfare.

Yamamoto's great gamble

All the same, the newspaper's confidence was far from unreasonable. Because it proved so outstandingly successful, we tend to forget just how risky Yamamoto's plan was. Any one of a hundred things might have gone wrong – but somehow didn't. Without last-minute solutions to the technical problems of high-level and torpedo-bombing, the mission would have been at best a partial success. The 3,000-mile trip had to be made without a single stray merchant vessel or plane observing the task force. If the weather had been bad enough to prevent refuelling of the ships, only a few could have gone all the way; if it had been bad enough to prevent take-off, there would not have been an attack at all. If the Americans had guessed right instead of wrong – if the Pacific Fleet had not been in port – if the radar report or the submarine sightings had been taken seriously . . . . There are so many *ifs* that it is possible to argue that Yamamoto's scheme was in fact ill-conceived, perhaps almost insane, and did have only "one chance in a million of being successful" – a judgement that might still be correct even if the million-to-one chance actually came off. At any rate, although it proved a mistake to believe that a direct, early Japanese attack on Pearl Harbor was not seriously in question, it was also a perfectly natural mistake to make.

A wealth of information

The United States government, including its War and Navy departments, thought along much the same lines, and, in spite of excellent information, made the same sort of mistakes. It had plenty of warnings that the Japanese were preparing to strike, since American cryptanalysts had broken "Purple", the high-level diplomatic code used by Tokyo to communicate with its embassies and consulates all over the world. For the delighted Americans this was "Operation Magic": it did not actually tell them the decisions made by the Japanese government, but they could now infer many of them from the decoded instructions. They knew, for example, that on 24th November the Japanese negotiators in Washington had been given until the 29th to reach a settlement with the USA; if they did not, "then things are automatically going to

The US machine that broke the high-level Japanese code, "Purple". Its operation ("Magic") provided information that might have alerted Americans to Japan's intended attack on Pearl Harbor.

happen" stated the Foreign Office in Tokyo. Later, they knew that Japanese diplomats in several key cities were being ordered to destroy their code books, machines and other "sensitive" documents – an action so drastic that it could only mean war was imminent, and with it the danger of police raids on the Japanese consulates and embassies. (In peacetime a country's embassy is normally outside the jurisdiction of the host nation's authorities.) Furthermore, by 5th December both the United States and Britain knew – from their observers in the field, not from "Magic" – that convoys of Japanese troop transports and warships were heading south for some unknown destination.

Roosevelt responsible?

So President Roosevelt and his advisers were certainly aware that the Japanese-American talks were highly unlikely to succeed, and that "things" were "automatically going to happen" – which clearly meant a Japanese aggression. A few historians have been so impressed by this that they have felt at a loss to explain Roosevelt's apparent inaction; some have even argued that the President knew about the planned Japanese attack on Pearl Harbor, but deliberately allowed it to happen so that the United States would be forced to enter the World War. However, there has never been any proper evidence to support this accusation, and it is based on an underestimation of the difficulties facing the President.

Where would the Japanese strike? In the first place, the Americans did not know where Japan would strike, or how directly their action would involve the United States. But they were fairly sure that the problem concerned targets in Asia. Almost all American intelligence reports in 1941 concentrated on Japanese moves to the north-west or south-west. A top-level example occurred in the joint memorandum to the President by General Marshall and his Navy counterpart, Admiral Stark, compiled on 27th November (the day they sent out the War Warnings): their long list of possible Japanese targets included the Soviet maritime ports but did not mention Pearl Harbor. So Roosevelt's preoccupation with Asia was shared by his military advisers; and here the American and British governments *had* acted energetically in an attempt to warn the Japanese off – the Americans by reinforcing the Philippines as fast as they could, and the British by sending two battleships, the ill-fated *Prince of Wales* and *Repulse*, to the Far East. This policy failed to change Japan's war-like plans, as the British and Americans realized when they spotted Japanese convoys travelling south-west. On the other hand, these sightings did seem to prove that American intelligence had been right – that the Japanese were interested in South-East Asia rather than the Pacific. No one anticipated that they would find the nerve and military resources to strike out in both directions at once.

The President's problems Even when the Japanese were known to be on the move, the President's course was not clear. If they attacked the Philippines or any US possession, war would certainly follow. If, however, the Japanese target was a British or Dutch colony, Roosevelt might find it harder to persuade Congress and public opinion that American interests were so strongly threatened that they should go to war. And if the Japanese only invaded Thailand, which did not belong to any of the colonial powers, Japanese-American relations might be broken off but war might still be avoided.

A passive policy Roosevelt's freedom of action was therefore limited: given the state of American opinion, there could be no question of attacking the Japanese first, however threatening their behaviour became. The President wanted Japan to strike the first blow so that he could bring a united American people into the war, and so that there could be no question about who had been the real aggressor. Marshall and Stark also wanted a passive American policy, for purely military reasons: their

53

joint memorandum stated that the build-up of strength in the Philippines was not yet complete, and advised the President to take "no action which might lead to immediate hostilities". They stressed that "The most essential thing now, from the United States viewpoint, is to gain time."

With all these preoccupations, and a wealth of advice all pointing in the same direction, it is hardly surprising that the President's thoughts were far from Pearl Harbor. After all, War Warnings *had* been sent out to all American commanders. The President might have been forgiven for thinking that he had done all he could to preserve peace and safeguard his country.

Vital clues ignored Yet the Americans did have some clues to Japanese intentions that might have led to a Pearl Harbor alert, if their significance had been realized. The most important clues were provided by "Magic" intercepts of coded exchanges between Tokyo and the Japanese consulate in Honolulu. Any run-of-the-mill spy-master would have asked for information about the installations at Pearl Harbor and the whereabouts of the Pacific Fleet; but the Japanese Foreign Office wanted much more. Their demand for precise and regular information to locate all the warships in the harbour had only two possible meanings: either Tokyo had become obsessed with information-gathering for its own sake (which is not unknown in intelligence organizations), or the Japanese were contemplating an attack. On 15th November the consulate was instructed to report twice-weekly instead of weekly, a message which might have suggested to an alert reader that an attack was imminent. But it didn't. "Purple" messages were decoded in huge quantities – such huge quantities that only a selected few were shown to the President and other leading figures. The vital clues were passed over and remained buried in mountains of paper.

Japan's revealing message The Americans' last chance to avoid disaster was also provided by "Magic". On the night of 6th-7th December, Washington time, the Japanese embassy in the city received a 14-point note from its government. This was Japan's final note to the United States, concluding with the words "The Japanese government regrets that it is impossible to reach agreement through further negotiations." As the message arrived in Purple code, US Naval Intelligence was able to decode it at the same time as the Japanese diplomats in Washington. Although the breaking-off of talks was serious,

Japanese diplomats Kurusu and Nomura waiting in US Secretary of State Cordell Hull's office to deliver Japan's final note. They did not know about the attack on Pearl Harbor, which was already in full swing.

the most interesting feature was Tokyo's instruction that the diplomats should deliver the note at *exactly* 1 p.m. – that is, at 7.30 a.m. Hawaiian time, half an hour before the attack on Pearl Harbor was scheduled to begin. This is said to have been done at Admiral Yamamoto's insistence, so that Japan should not be accused of having launched a "sneak attack", though the note was not a declaration of war – and the Japanese task force's prearranged trip across the Pacific hardly constituted "fair play"! The Japanese diplomats were also ordered to destroy their code machines.

How the last chance was missed

Four hours before the attack, an alert Naval Intelligence officer read the instruction and realized that the very unusual emphasis on timing must be highly significant. There followed a tragi-comedy of delays and accidents. Admiral Stark realized the importance of the message, but saw no point in issuing yet another War Warning: he believed that the Pacific Fleet was already on the alert. General Marshall was out riding. When he was finally contacted, he decided that it *was* worth sending a new warning. Stark rang to say he would "go along with" this, and offered the use of naval radio. Marshall preferred to use the army's equipment. From noon his warning went out to the Caribbean and the Philippines, but atmospherics blocked the line to Hawaii. A subordinate sent the message – by the ordinary commercial service, Western Union.

Marshall had written JUST WHAT SIGNIFICANCE THE HOUR SET MAY HAVE WE DO NOT KNOW BUT BE ON ALERT ACCORDINGLY. INFORM NAVAL AUTHORITIES OF THIS COMMUNICATION.

No one can say whether Short and Kimmel would have acted promptly or effectively enough if they had received the cable in time. In the event, it was not delivered until 11:45, Hawaiian time, amid the chaos following the attack, by a Japanese-Hawaiian messenger who reached army headquarters by bicycle.

US Army Chief of Staff General George C. Marshall. Some writers believe that Marshall was partly to blame for American unpreparedness at Pearl Harbor. After the Second World War, Marshall sponsored a scheme for massive US aid ("the Marshall Plan") that helped the ruined European economy to recover.

Who won at Pearl Harbor?

Raising the Oklahoma. *Although sunk in Pearl Harbor, the ship was successfully salvaged, reconditioned and put back into service.*

It is possible to argue that, despite its spectacular results, the attack on Pearl Harbor was not entirely successful. One of its drawbacks was built into the scheme: it enraged and united the Americans, so that Roosevelt had no difficulty in mobilizing American forces and putting the great industries of the United States on a war footing. The attack itself was arguably mishandled in that the Japanese concentrated too much on the American battleships, leaving almost untouched the fuel tanks, machine shops and other installations at Pearl

Harbor, which were equally vital sinews of war. (In fact, although it would be wrong to underestimate the damage inflicted by the Japanese, it remains true that only two of the US battleships were completely lost: the rest eventually returned to service after salvage and repair operations.) Most important of all, the Japanese failed to seek out and destroy the American carriers, even though their own exploits were demonstrating that the carrier was now the decisive vessel in Pacific warfare. This was primarily the fault of the task force commander, Nagumo, who had no experience of air warfare and had never favoured the Pearl Harbor scheme. Psychological considerations probably played their part too. Having nerved himself to accept heavy losses, Nagumo found that his task force had got off scot-free; the temptation not to repeat the risk was evidently overwhelming, and Nagumo took his ships straight back to Japan, even dispensing with an earlier-planned raid-in-passing on Midway.

Japan "runs wild"

Nevertheless, Nagumo was right in arguing that the attack had achieved its main object – to buy time. Over the next few

Japanese soldiers march into Singapore after its surrender. Winston Churchill called this "the worst disaster and largest capitulation in British history". Some 70,000 British and Commonwealth servicemen became Japanese prisoners of war.

months Japan overran the Philippines, the Dutch East Indies, Thailand, Malaysia and most of Burma. Japanese forces also pushed out into the Pacific, through the Marianas, Marshalls and Gilberts, capturing Wake and the other American bases. The aim was not to defeat the United States but to create a defensive perimeter far out in the Pacific that could be held indefinitely against the Americans, or else taken by them at such enormous cost that they would recoil and make a negotiated peace with Japan. In possession of an enormous empire stretching from Burma to the Marshalls, Japan's rulers might well have believed that this was perfectly possible.

The inevitability of defeat

The Japanese heavy cruiser Mikuma, *destroyed by American dive-bombers at the end of the battle of Midway, June 1942. This began as a Japanese offensive and turned into a catastrophe for the Imperial Navy.*

Britain's leader, Winston Churchill, knew better. On the night after Pearl Harbor he reflected that "We had won the war. England would live . . .". He realized that the enormous strength of the United States ensured a victorious outcome to the war, though it might take a long time to defeat both the Japanese and their European allies. Like other militarists – including Hitler and Mussolini – the Japanese leaders made the mistake of considering more peaceful peoples "soft", only to be surprised by the determination they showed when once they were roused.

A setting sun

Appropriately enough, the first clear turning point in the Pacific war was the battle of Midway in June 1942 – appropriately because this naval battle was largely won by "Magic", of whose existence the Japanese were still not aware, and because it involved the destruction of four Japanese carriers, all of them veterans of the Pearl Harbor attack. Although hard campaigns were fought in China and Burma, the main theatres of the war were in the Pacific and involved extensive naval or amphibious operations. In a punishing three-year campaign the Allies landed in the Solomon Islands, fought their way along the coast of New Guinea and eventually recaptured most of the Philippines. In the Pacific, the US Navy and Marines captured one Japanese base after another in a brilliantly successful "island hopping" campaign.

The Japanese fought fiercely, but every encounter weakened them, since the United States could quickly replace her material losses and they could not. In the air, the loss of Japan's experienced flyers – including most of the victors of Pearl Harbor – rendered the remaining Japanese carriers useless and left her other ships defenceless against Allied air attacks. Admiral Yamamoto did not live to see the end of the Imperial Navy: the Americans intercepted a radio message

The USS Tennessee, back in action after being damaged during the Japanese attack on Pearl Harbor; here it is bombarding Okinawa just before the assault on 1st April, 1944. In the foreground, amphibious vehicles (Amtracks) carry US Marines to the beachheads.

which gave information about a flight he was making, and in April 1943 his plane was shot down. Two battles in 1944 completed the ruin of the Imperial Navy. When the Americans finally invaded one of the Japanese home islands, Okinawa, the remnants of the Japanese Navy sailed to the rescue, provided with only enough fuel for a one-way trip. It was a suicide mission that had little chance of even reaching its target (the American troop transports); without air cover, the Japanese vessels were pulverized and sent to the bottom.

The kamikazes

Kamikaze pilots being briefed before an attack. These inexperienced flyers knew they were going to their deaths: their mission was to destroy enemy vessels by crashing explosive-packed aircraft into them.

From first to last, Japan's resistance was prolonged by her soldiers' willingness to die. In one action after another the Japanese fought to the last man, while their defeated commanders committed *hara-kiri* rather than be taken prisoner. But it was the airmen who made a final effort to avoid the unthinkable defeat, acting in the same spirit as the flyers who had been prepared to crash through torpedo netting at Pearl Harbor. Young men who knew little more than how to fly their planes, would take them up, loaded with explosives, and crash them into US warships. They were

called *kamikazes*, after the "divine wind" that had saved Japan almost seven centuries earlier.

The most frightful weapon

The *kamikazes* did considerable damage, but by this time American superiority was too great for their operations to affect the issue. However, the war *was* ended by attacks from

Devastated Hiroshima after the dropping of the atom bomb on 6th August, 1945.

the air. Deciding that an invasion of Japan would cost too many Allied lives, the American President, Harry S. Truman (Roosevelt had died), authorized the use of a frightful new secret weapon. On 14th August 1945, after atomic bombs had been dropped on Hiroshima and Nagasaki, Japan surrendered and the Second World War came to an end.

Further reading

THE EVENTS

Gordon W. Prange, *At Dawn We Slept: The Untold Story of Pearl Harbor*, Michael Joseph, 1982. (An excellent but dauntingly long and detailed study.)

THE INVESTIGATION

General
John Costello, *The Pacific War*, Revised edition, Pan Books, 1985
James L. Stokesbury, *A Short History of World War II*, Hale, 1982
John Toland, *Infamy: Pearl Harbor and Its Aftermath*, Methuen, 1982. (The most recent "revisionist" work, arguing that Roosevelt knew of the impending attack. Should only be read in conjunction with Costello and Prange.)

Japanese history and culture
Richard Tames, *Japan in the Twentieth Century*, Batsford, 1981

Personalities
John Deane Potter, *Admiral of the Pacific: The Life of Yamamoto*, Heinemann, 1963
Michael Rawcliffe, *The Roosevelt File*, Batsford, 1980

Index